D1466415

DISCARDED

From Nashville Public Library

NPL|F

Nashville Public Library | FOUNDATION

*This book given
to the Nashville Public Library
through the generosity of the*
**Dollar General
Literacy Foundation**

NPLF.ORG

DAY BY DAY WITH...

BEYONCÉ

BY
TAMMY GAGNE

PUBLISHERS
P.O. Box 196
Hockessin, Delaware 19707
Visit us on the web: www.mitchelllane.com

Mitchell Lane
PUBLISHERS

Copyright © 2016 by Mitchell Lane Publishers, Inc. All rights reserved. No part of this book may be reproduced without written permission from the publisher. Printed and bound in the United States of America.

Printing   1   2   3   4   5   6   7   8   9

RANDY'S CORNER
DAY BY DAY WITH. . .

Adam Jones	Justin Bieber
Alex Morgan	LeBron James
Beyoncé	Manny Machado
Bindi Sue Irwin	Mia Hamm
Calvin Johnson	Miley Cyrus
Carrie Underwood	Missy Franklin
Chloë Moretz	Selena Gomez
Dwayne "The Rock" Johnson	Serena Williams
Elena Delle Donne	Shakira
Eli Manning	Shaun White
Gabby Douglas	Stephen Hillenburg
Jennifer Lopez	Taylor Swift
	Willow Smith

Library of Congress Cataloging-in-Publication Data
Gagne, Tammy.
Day by day with Beyoncé / by Tammy Gagne.
    pages cm. — (Randy's corner)
Includes bibliographical references and index.
ISBN 978-1-68020-109-3 (library bound)
1. Beyoncé, 1981– —Juvenile literature. 2. Rhythm and blues musicians—United States—Biography—Juvenile literature. 3. Singers—United States—Biography—Juvenile literature. I. Title.
ML3930.K66G34 2016
782.42164092—dc23
[B]
                                                          2015017402
eBook ISBN: 978-1-68020-110-9

ABOUT THE AUTHOR: Tammy Gagne has written dozens of books for children, including *Adele* and *Ke$ha* for Mitchell Lane Publishers. She resides in northern New England with her husband and son. One of her favorite pastimes is visiting schools to speak to kids about the writing process.

PUBLISHER'S NOTE: The following story has been thoroughly researched and to the best of our knowledge represents a true story. While every possible effort has been made to ensure accuracy, the publisher will not assume liability for damages caused by inaccuracies in the data, and makes no warranty on the accuracy of the information contained herein. This story has not been authorized or endorsed by Beyoncé.

GRA

BEYONCÉ POSES AT THE VH1 DIVAS DUETS AT THE MGM GRAND HOTEL IN LAS VEGAS, NEVADA.

Talented singer and actress. Wife, mother, sister, and daughter. Beyoncé is all of these things and more. She rose to fame in the late 1990s as part of the female rhythm and blues group Destiny's Child. And her success continues to grow.

MICHELLE WILLIAMS, KELLY ROWLAND AND BEYONCÉ SING "SAY YES" AT THE 30TH ANNUAL STELLAR AWARDS.

Today the singer known as Queen B was born
Beyoncé Giselle Knowles on September 4,
1981. She grew up near Houston, Texas, the
daughter of Mathew and Tina Knowles.
Matthew was a successful Xerox salesman.
Beyoncé's mother owned a hair salon, where
young Beyoncé once worked sweeping the
floor.

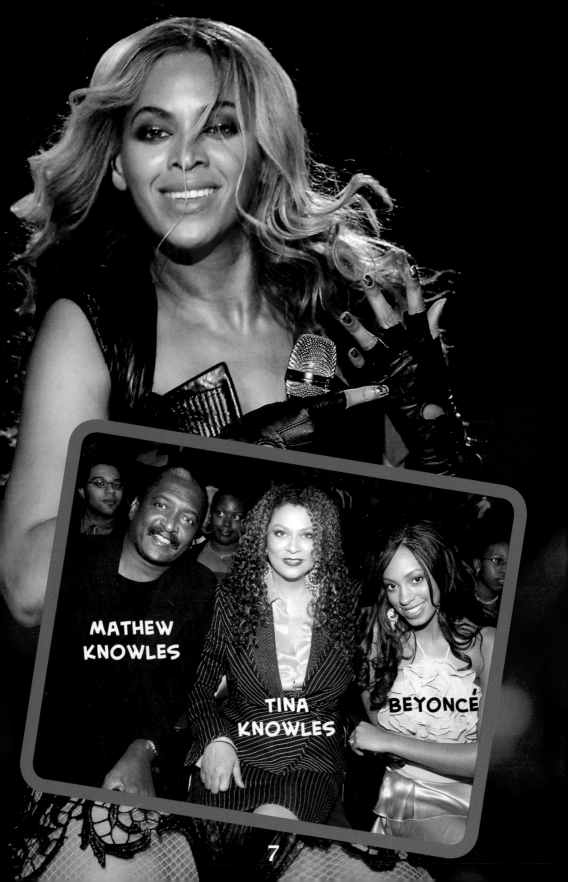

MATHEW
KNOWLES

TINA
KNOWLES

BEYONCÉ

BEYONCÉ ARRIVES AT THE 81ST ANNUAL ACADEMY AWARDS IN LOS ANGELES, CALIFORNIA.

Beyoncé loved going to Six Flags theme park when she was a child. She would often sing for tips at her mother's salon to pay for her season pass. Her younger sister Solange also enjoyed singing. They regularly put on shows together.

Even as a young girl, Beyoncé knew she wanted to sing for a living. She began competing in talent shows. In 1993, she appeared on the ABC television show *Star Search* with a group called Gyrls Tyme. Sadly, the girls lost to a rock band called Skeleton Crew.

BEYONCÉ KNOWLES

KELLY ROWLAND

MICHELLE WILLIAMS

Beyoncé didn't let that setback get in the way of success. Her father believed that Gyrls Tyme was destined for success. He was so certain in fact that he quit his job to become the girls' manager. It was around that time that they changed their name to Destiny's Child.

In 1997, Destiny's Child released a song called "Killing Time." It appeared on the *Men in Black* movie soundtrack. They also recorded their first album titled "Destiny's Child" with Columbia Records. It sold more than a million copies.

JAY-Z

Beyoncé's career wasn't the only thing blossoming for the young star. She also fell in love with rising hip-hop star Jay-Z Carter. Neither was in a hurry to get married. "We took our time and developed an unbreakable friendship before we got married," Beyoncé told *Harper's Bazaar* magazine.

Soon Destiny's Child was the top female singing group in the world. But Beyoncé still wanted something more. In 2003, she recorded her first solo album *Dangerously in Love*. Columbia Records wasn't sure it would

sell. "They told me I didn't have one single on my album," Beyoncé told *Billboard Magazine* in 2011. "I guess they were kind of right," she added. "I had five."

BEYONCÉ POSING WITH HER AWARD FROM THE AMERICAN MUSIC AWARDS IN LOS ANGELES, CALIFORNIA

19

After Beyoncé had conquered the music world, it was time to move on to the silver screen. She began her acting career playing Foxxy Cleopatra in *Goldmember*, the third movie in the *Austin Powers* comedy series. But it was her role in *Dreamgirls* that proved she could be a serious actress.

BILL CONDON (DIRECTOR), JAMIE FOXX, BEYONCÉ, DANNY GLOVER, AND JENNIFER HUDSON

MIKE MYERS

BEYONCÉ

21

BEYONCÉ POSES WITH JAY-Z AT THE METROPOLITAN MUSEUM OF ART IN NEW YORK CITY.

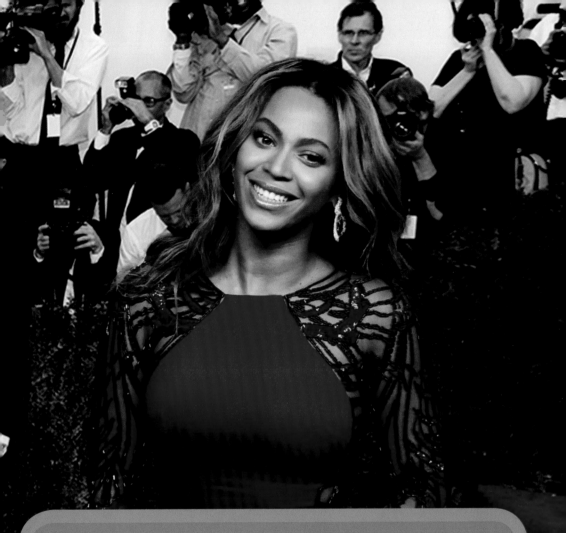

After dating for nearly a decade, Beyoncé and Jay-Z were finally ready to walk down the aisle. They married in a small ceremony in New York City on April 4, 2008. The same year she became a married woman, Beyoncé released a song called "All the Single Ladies." It became one of her biggest hits.

BLUE IVY

24

The couple welcomed daughter Blue Ivy on January 7, 2012. "It was the best day of my life," she told London's *Daily Mail* newspaper. When describing the joy her husband and child give her, Beyoncé said, "Those are the things that matter, and at this point in my life that's what I'm striving for—growth, love, happiness, fun."

Young girls see Beyoncé as a role model for all that she has accomplished. But people who know her best are inspired by her genuine character. Friend Gwyneth Paltrow told *Harper's Bazaar,* "B is wise beyond her years. She has taught me the value of speaking your mind. She is clear and honest and true to herself while being respectful."

Beyoncé has also shown her character through her charity work. She has given more than $7 million dollars to the Knowles-Temenos Place Apartments in Houston. The complex provides shelter for dozens of people. The facility also provides meals, job training, and other services to help the down-on-their-luck residents get back on their feet.

DONATE HERE! 29

No one knows what the future holds for this superstar. But chances are good that Beyoncé still has a fair amount of success ahead of her. She takes life as it comes. As

she told *Marie Claire* magazine, "I don't have to prove anything to anyone, I only have to follow my heart and concentrate on what I want to say to the world. I run my world."

FURTHER READING

FIND OUT MORE

Dann, Sarah. *Beyoncé*. New York: Crabtree Publishing, 2013.

Landau, Elaine. *Beyoncé: R&B Superstar*. Minneapolis: Lerner Publishing Group, 2012.

Schuman, Michael A. *Beyoncé: A Biography of a Legendary Singer*. Berkeley Heights, NJ: Enslow, 2014.

WORKS CONSULTED

Alexander, Cheryl. "Behind the Music—the business empire of Matthew Knowles." *Houston Lifestyles and Homes*. March 1, 2013. http://houstonlifestyles.com/mathew-knowles/

Andrews, Marc. "Nothing feels like my child singing 'mummy' . . . nothing feels like when I look my husband in the eyes! Beyoncé talks family." *Daily Mail*. December 18, 2013. http://www.dailymail.co.uk/tvshowbiz/article-2525810/Beyonce-talks-family-Nothing-feels-like-child-singing-mummy-feels-like-I-look-husband-eyes.html

Betiku, Fehintola, Jade Watkins, and Lucy Buckland. "'Blue Ivy is my road dog, my homey, my best friend': Beyoncé reveals unique connection with baby daughter 'which developed during pregnancy.'" *Daily Mail*. February 12, 2013. http://www.dailymail.co.uk/tvshowbiz/article-2277556/Beyonce-reveals-unique-connection-baby-Blue-Ivy-developed-pregnancy.html

Couch, Robbie. "Beyoncé Has Quietly Given $7 Million to Homeless in Hometown of Houston." *Huffington Post*. July 9, 2014. http://www.huffingtonpost.com/2014/07/09/beyonce-hometown-houston_n_5570609.html

Jones, Nate. "Skeleton Crew: Meet the Band Who Beat a Young Beyoncé on Star Search." *People.com*. December 22, 2013. http://www.people.com/people/article/0,,20768720,00.html

Lipsky-Karasz. Elisa. "Beyoncé's Baby Love." *Harper's Bazaar*. October 2011. http://www.harpersbazaar.com/celebrity/news/beyonces-baby-love-interview-1111

Rice, Francesca. "Beyoncé: 20 Quotes From The Most Powerful Celebrity In The World." *Marie Claire*. September 4, 2014. http://www.marieclaire.co.uk/blogs/545716/bow-down-bitches-15-beyonce-quotes-that-cemented-her-place-as-one-of-the-most-inspiring-women-ever.html

Robinson, Melia. "What Beyoncé Has Accomplished in 32 Years is Mind-Blowing." *Business Insider*. September 4, 2013. http://www.businessinsider.com/how-beyonce-became-famous-2013-9?op=1

ON THE INTERNET

Beyoncé—Official Web Site
http://www.beyonce.com/
Knowles-Temenos Place Apartments
http://www.temenoscdc.org/

INDEX

PHOTO CREDITS: pp. 4—© Sbukley | Dreamstime.com; pp 5—Erik Umphery/Getty Images for Parkwood Entertainment; pp. 6-7—Chris Graythen/Getty Images; pp. 7—Frank Micelotta & Staff/Getty Images; pp. 8—Kevork Djansezian/Getty Images; p. 9—Michael Tran/FilmMagic; pp. 10-11—Jason Kempin/Getty Images; pp 12—Peter Brooker/REX/Newscom; pp. 13—PHOTOG/IPOL/Globe Photos,INC.; pp. 14-15—DAVID TULIS/UPI/Newscom; pp. 16-17—AP Photo/Luca Bruno; p. 18—Kevin Winter/ImageDirect; p. 19—© Carrienelson1 | Dreamstime.com; p. 20—Tony Barson/WireImage; p. 21—IPOL/Globe Photos, INC.; pp. 22-23—Patrick McMullan Co./McMullan/Sipa USA/Newscom; pp. 24-25—MARIO ANZUONI/REUTERS/Newscom; pp. 26-27—LUCY NICHOLSON/REUTERS/Newscom; p.28-29 - Raymond Boyd/GettyImages; p. 30— Frank Micelotta/Getty Images; p. 31—Frederick M. Brown/Getty Images;